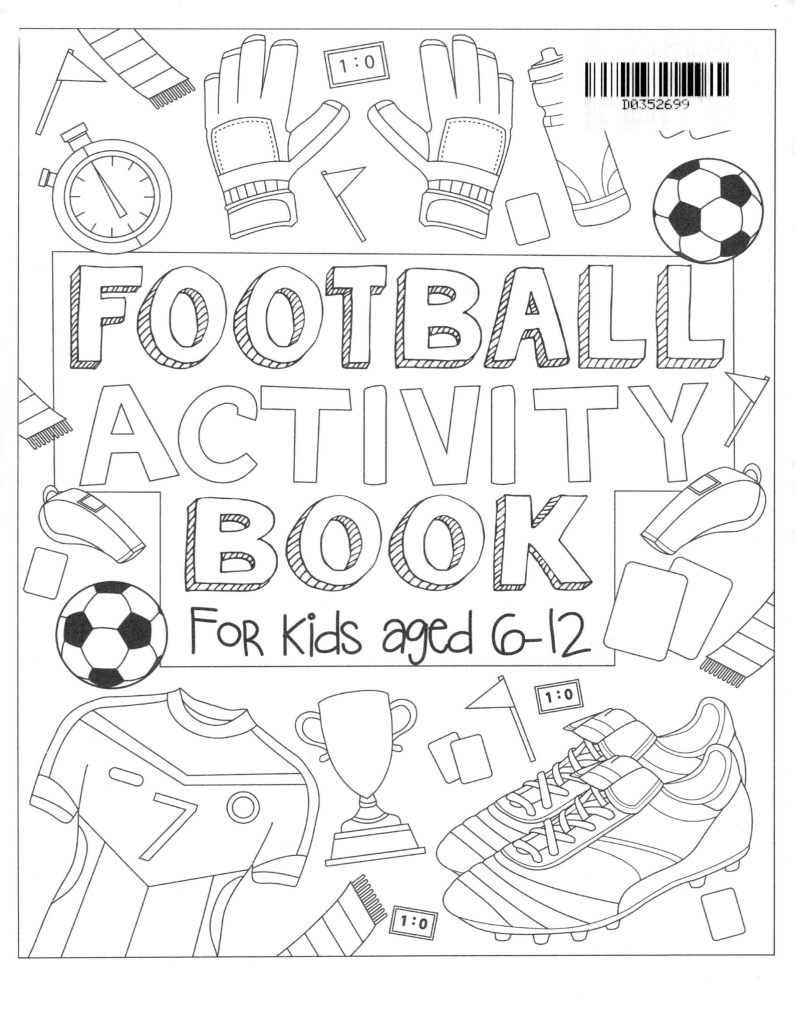

FOOTBALL ACTIVITY BOOK

For kids aged 6-12

Published in 2018 by The Future Teacher Foundation

© The Future Teacher Foundation

www.thefutureteacherfoundation.com

ISBN-13: 978-1727550238

ISBN-10: 1727550234

For printing and manufacturing information please see the last page.

If you choose to remove pages for framing, ask an adult to carefully extract with a scalpel and ruler.

Warning: This book is not suitable for children under 36 months of age due to potential small parts - choking hazard.

This book belongs to...

_____

Spot the 11 differences between these two pictures.
Colour the picture when you have found them all!

Colour this page any way you like!

Fill in this A-Z of famous footballer names.

First name or surname must begin with each letter of the alphabet.

1 POINT FOR EACH PLAYER YOU CAN NAME.

A. _____

B. _____

C. _____

D. _____

E. _____

F. _____

G. _____

H. _____

I. _____

J. _____

K. _____

L. _____

M. _____

N. _____

O. _____

P. _____

Q. _____

R. _____

S. _____

T. _____

U. _____

V. _____

W. _____

X. _____

Y. _____

Z. _____

Find the pairs of football shirts.

When you find a pair draw a circle around each one,
and then a line that joins the pair.

NOW COLOUR THE SHIRTS IF YOU WANT TO!

Can you find the football words in this word search?

W	O	H	S	I	R	F	D	E	G
H	R	E	F	E	R	E	E	H	O
U	S	A	V	E	M	D	K	M	A
P	I	T	C	H	C	E	G	A	L
B	A	L	O	F	S	F	O	N	G
A	I	A	R	A	H	E	A	A	K
L	H	B	N	M	O	N	T	G	S
L	T	Y	E	S	T	D	U	E	N
A	S	T	R	I	K	E	R	R	A
W	S	C	O	R	E	R	T	H	F

PITCH   SCORE   STRIKER   DEFENDER

BALL   REFEREE   SHOT   MANAGER

GOAL   CORNER   SAVE   FANS

Design your ultimate football boots.

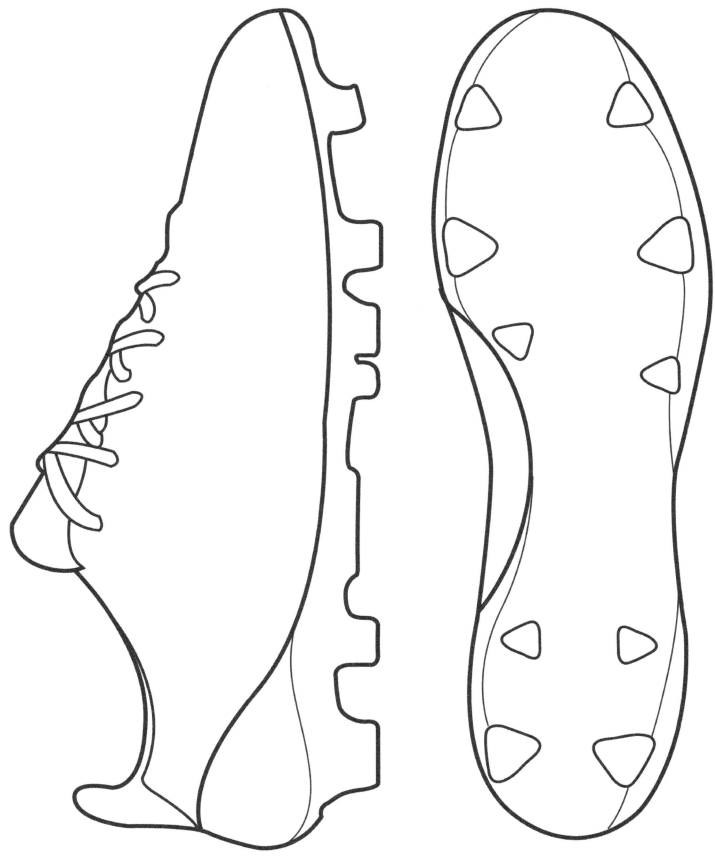

Can you solve these famous footballer anagrams?

You must try and work out who the professional footballer is.
For a bonus point can you write what teams they play for?

COLOUR THE SHIRTS WHEN YOU ARE DONE!

ssemi 10

bmppea 7

orndola 7

_ _ _ _ _ _ _

_ _ _ _ _ _ _ _

_ _ _ _ _ _ _

ed age 1

ekna 9

ramney 10

_ _ _ _ _ _ _

_ _ _ _ _ _ _ _

_ _ _ _ _ _ _

Who is your favourite outfield professional football player?

Draw their face, colour them in and then give them a score out of 100 for their skills.

Player's Name...

Heading

Shooting

Pace

Tackling

Stamina

Control

Set Pieces

Physical Strength

Dribbling

Passing

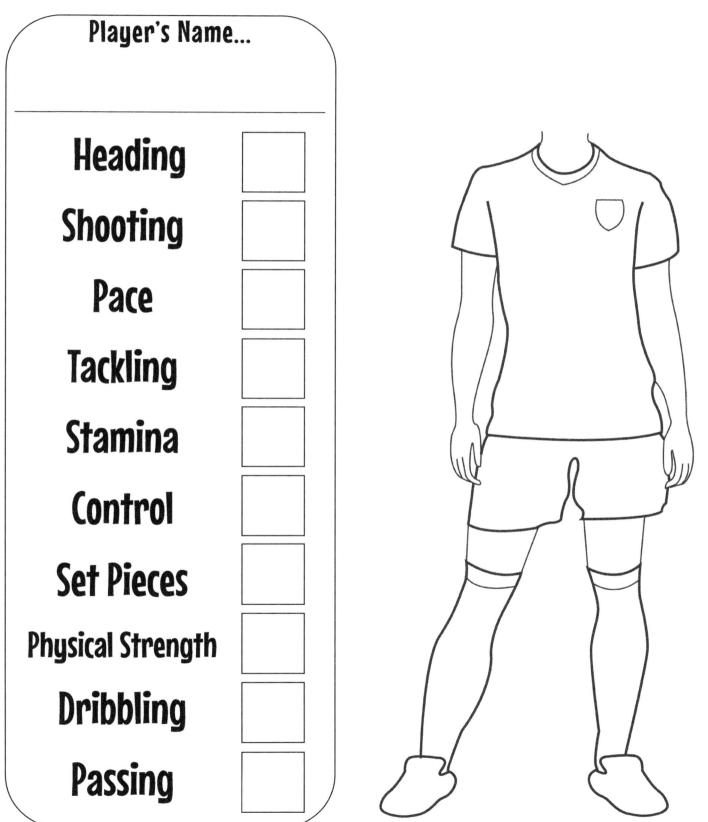

Colour this picture of a professional footballer...

Add patterns, designs and colour to these goalie gloves.

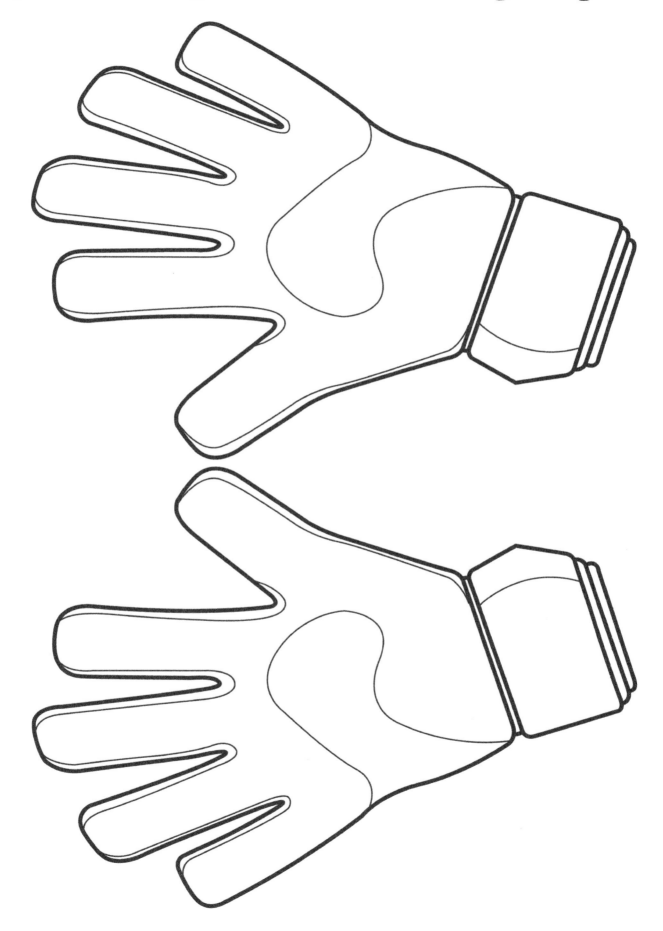

Soccer silhouettes!
Draw your own soccer silhouettes below!

My football skills: assessment and targets.

Give yourself a score out of 100 for your football skills.
See what you need to develop and then work on those areas.

Picture of me...

My position on the pitch...

What skills am I best at?

What do I need to improve?

Skill	Score
Heading	
Shooting	
Pace	
Tackling	
Stamina	
Control	
Set Pieces	
Physical Strength	
Dribbling	
Passing	
Goalkeeping	

Colour this page any way you like!

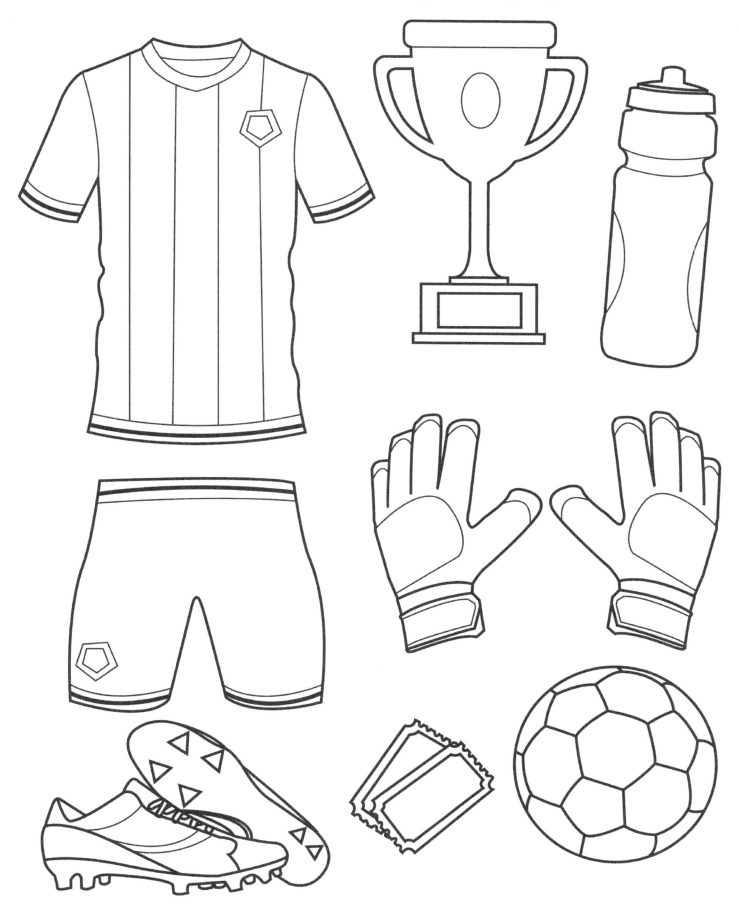

Design and colour a new emblem for your team.

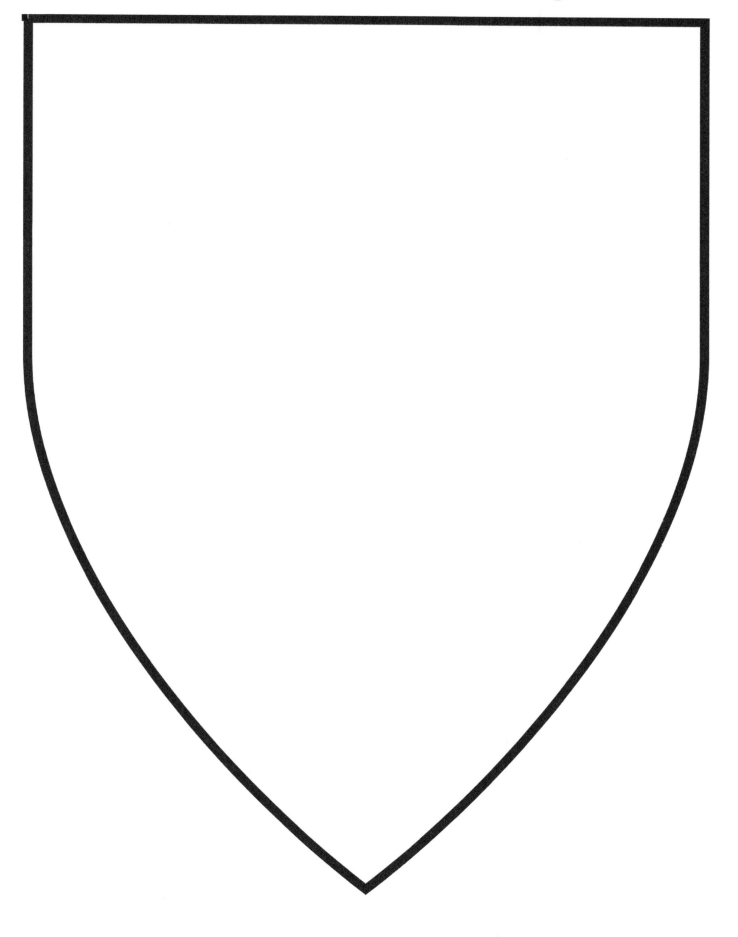

Football teams A-Z.

Can you name 26 professional football teams from around the World?

1 POINT FOR EACH TEAM YOU CAN NAME!

A. _____

B. _____

C. _____

D. _____

E. _____

F. _____

G. _____

H. _____

I. _____

J. _____

K. _____

L. _____

M. _____

N. _____

O. _____

P. _____

Q. _____

R. _____

S. _____

T. _____

U. _____

V. _____

W. _____

X. _____

Y. _____

Z. _____

Football fans' faces!

Football fans feel all sorts of feelings when supporting their team.

Draw a face in each box that shows how a fan would feel when...

Losing a cup final on penalties.	Signing an awesome new player.
Winning the league.	**Seeing a bad refereeing decision.**

Design a cool new football kit for a team you love.

Football fun!!!

Use the empty pages in this book or just have fun thinking about these cool activities.

1. Make up a new chant or song for fans of your team to sing at a match.

2. Design a new away kit for your favourite team.

3. Design a cool set piece trick or routine to fool your opposition.

4. Create football cards of you and your friends.

5. Make up a new celebration dance or routine for your next goal.

6. Plan a new way to score a penalty that you can try out.

7. Pretend you are a manager and set out your best 1 – 11 of your favourite team – don't forget a winning formation too!

8. Write a list, in order, of your top 10, 20 or even 100 best pro players ever.

9. Design the ultimate football freestyle trick routine.

10. Plan out a football training session that will help you to develop your skills.

11. Imagine you are a football journalist and write down a few questions you'd love to ask your favourite player.

12. Plan out your ultimate, dream goal that you'd love to score.

Design a new scarf and beanie hat for a team you love!

Don't worry if you think you aren't a good artist, just do your best and have fun!

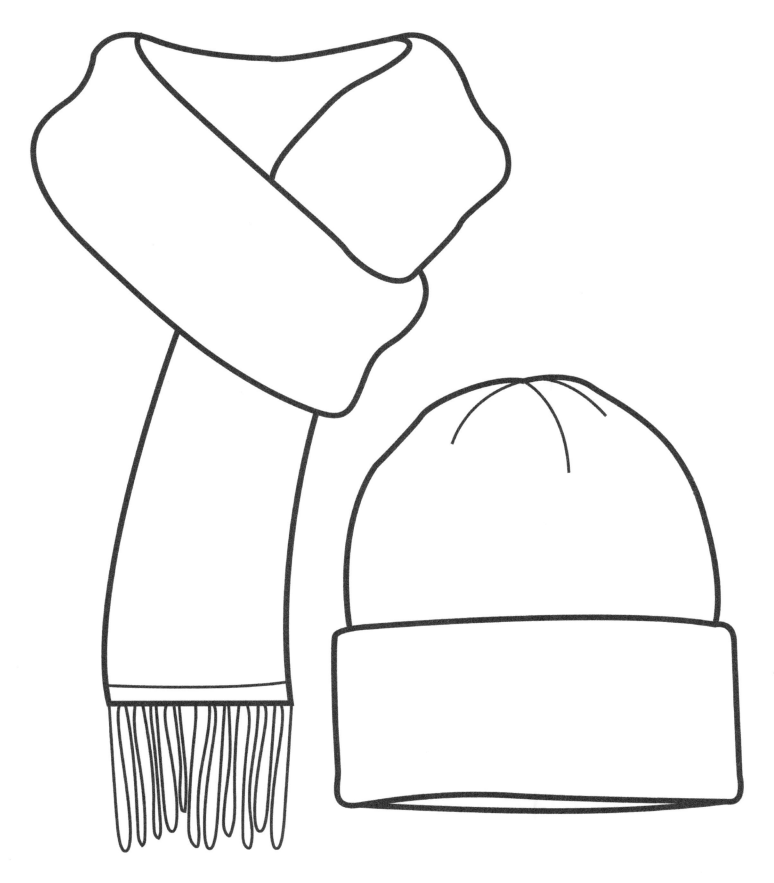

Use the grid to copy this picture.

Look closely and then copy the picture from the grid onto the other side.

Don't worry if it looks a bit tricky – just do your best and have fun!

NOW COLOUR THE PICTURES IF YOU WANT TO!

Can you find the international teams in this word search?

B	H	G	C	R	O	A	T	I	A
R	O	E	H	A	I	T	A	L	Y
A	D	R	I	N	W	C	P	O	D
Z	L	M	P	C	A	H	O	C	N
I	F	A	S	E	L	I	R	H	A
L	R	N	T	S	E	M	T	I	L
P	A	Y	A	P	S	E	U	L	T
E	N	G	L	A	N	D	G	E	O
L	C	R	O	I	U	S	A	F	C
A	E	N	G	N	B	R	L	P	S

ENGLAND   **USA**   **GERMANY**   **ITALY**

SPAIN   **CROATIA**   **WALES**   **CHILE**

FRANCE   **BRAZIL**   **SCOTLAND**   **PORTUGAL**

Your ultimate, fantasy football professional dream team.

No rules! You pick any player who has ever lived, in any formation...

TEAM NAME

TEAM LOGO

MANAGER

SUBS

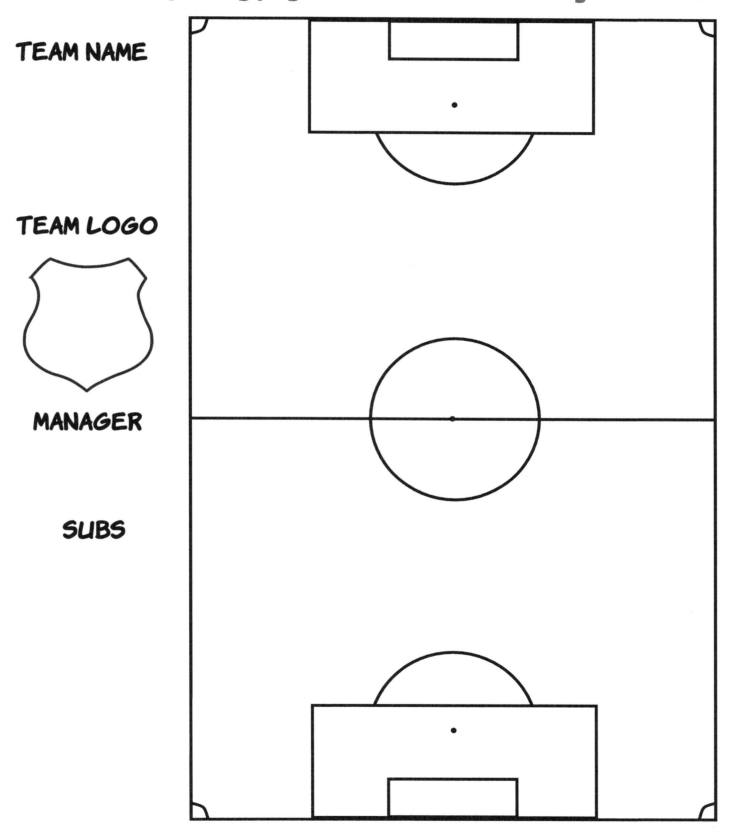

Design the cover of a brand new football video game!

Don't worry if you think you aren't a good artist, just do your best and have fun!

Play football hangman with someone...

A B C D E F G H I J K L M N O P Q R S T U V W X Y Z

A B C D E F G H I J K L M N O P Q R S T U V W X Y Z

Design a new ball for the World Cup.

Don't worry if you think you aren't a good artist, just do your best and have fun!

Give your new ball a name...

Draw and colour a comic strip of the best goal you've ever scored.
You can add words, speech and thought bubbles if you like...

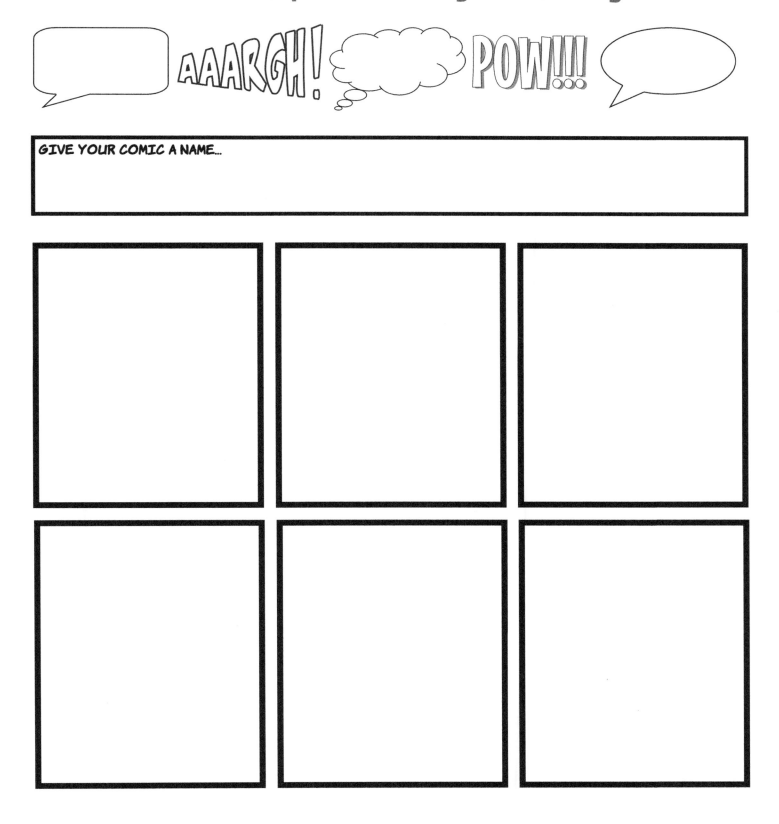

GIVE YOUR COMIC A NAME...

Draw and colour an awesome new trophy and medal.

 Decide if it is for a team or a player and add that information to the trophy and the medal.

Your favourite formations.

Plot out your favourite formations using black dots for each position.

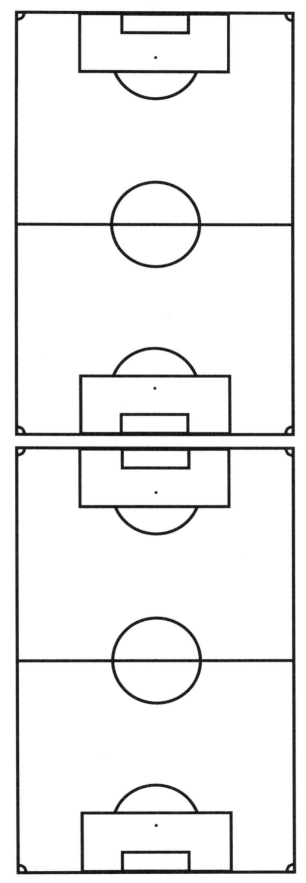

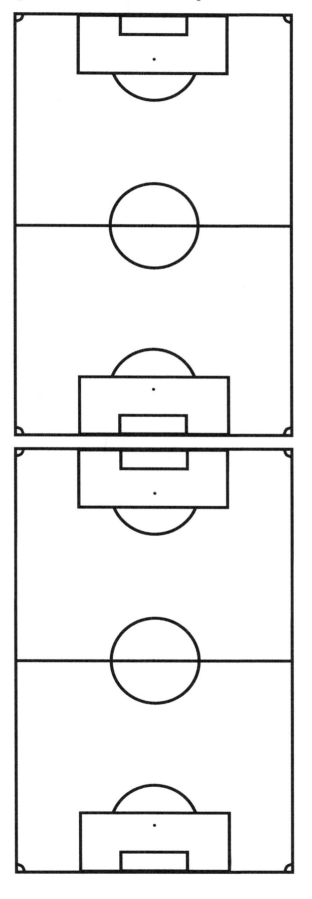

Design the cover of a match day program.
It can be for your favourite team or for a team you play for.

Printed in Great Britain
by Amazon

32763452R00038